D0894469

Symbols of American Freedom

Mount Rushmore

by William David Thomas

Series Consultant: Jerry D. Thompson,
Regents Professor of History,
Texas A&M International University

CHELSEA
CLUBHOUSE

An Imprint of Chelsea House Publishers

Symbols of American Freedom: Mount Rushmore

Chelsea Clubhouse
An imprint of Chelsea House Publishers
132 West 31st Street
New York NY 10001

Library of Congress Cataloging-in-Publication Data
Thomas, William, 1947-
      Mount Rushmore / by William David Thomas.
          p. cm. — (Symbols of American freedom)
      Includes index.
      ISBN 978-1-60413-515-2
      1. Mount Rushmore National Memorial (S.D.)—Juvenile literature. I. Title. II. Series.
  F657.R8T47 2010
  978.3'93—dc22
                                                    2009013027

Chelsea Clubhouse books are available at special discounts when purchased in bulk quantities for businesses, associations, institutions, or sales promotions. Please call our Special Sales Department in New York at (212) 967-8800 or (800) 322-8755.

You can find Chelsea Clubhouse on the World Wide Web at http://www.chelseahouse.com

Developed for Chelsea House by RJF Publishing LLC (www.RJFpublishing.com)
Text and cover design by Tammy West/Westgraphix LLC
Maps by Stefan Chabluk
Photo research by Edward A. Thomas
Index by Nila Glikin

Photo Credits: cover: Shutterstock Images; 5: Grant Faint/Photographer's Choice/Photolibrary; 6, 19, 25, 41: AP/Wide World Photos; 8, 30: © Underwood & Underwood/CORBIS; 11: © Thomas R. Fletcher/Alamy; 12: Glen Allison/Photodisc/Photolibray; 13: Private Collection/Peter Newark American Pictures/The Bridgeman Art Library; 15: agefotostock/Super Stock; 17, 22, 23, 37: National Park Service/Mount Rushmore National Memorial; 26: Library of Congress LC-USZ62-121165; 29: © INTERFOTO Pressebildagentur/Alamy; 33: National Geographic/Getty Images; 34: National Park Service; 36: © Bettmann/CORBIS; 39: First Light/agefotostock; 42: Corbis RF/agefotostock.

Printed and bound in the United States of America

Bang RJF 10 9 8 7 6 5 4 3 2 1

This book is printed on acid-free paper.

Note: Quotations in the text are used essentially as originally written. In some cases, spelling, punctuation, and the like have been modernized to aid student understanding.

Table of Contents

Words that are defined in the Glossary are in **bold** type
the first time they appear in the text.

The Importance of Mount Rushmore

Route 16A in South Dakota twists and turns through mountains. The road goes into a dark, rocky tunnel. As you come out of the tunnel, you can see four huge white faces. The walls of tunnel are like a picture frame around them. You are looking at Mount Rushmore National **Memorial**.

11-Foot Eyes

The faces of four U.S. presidents are carved into the mountain. George Washington and Thomas Jefferson are there. So are Abraham Lincoln and Theodore Roosevelt. Together, these four faces make up one of the largest **sculptures** in the world.

From the road, the faces look big. From a distance, however, it is hard to tell how big they really are. The cliff on which they are carved is more than 1,000 feet (305 meters) wide. Each of Washington's eyes is 11 feet (3.4 meters) across. His mouth is 18 feet

The sculpture on Mount Rushmore is one of the largest in the world. Carved into the mountainside are the faces of (from left to right) Presidents George Washington, Thomas Jefferson, Theodore Roosevelt, and Abraham Lincoln.

(5.5 meters) wide. From the top of Washington's head to the bottom of his chin is 60 feet (18.3 meters). That's as high as a six-story building.

Visitors are usually amazed at the size of the **monument**. Even presidents can be surprised. President Franklin D. Roosevelt visited Mount

A worker cleaning Washington's face looks tiny compared to the huge sculpture. From forehead to chin, Washington's head is 60 feet high.

Rushmore in the summer of 1936. (Theodore Roosevelt was his distant cousin.) When he saw the mountain, Franklin Roosevelt said:

> "I had seen the photographs, I had seen the drawings, and I had talked with those who are responsible for this great work, and yet I had no conception, until about ten minutes ago, not only of its magnitude, but also its permanent beauty and importance."

Miners, Buffalo, and Tourists

When the monument was started in the 1920s, the area was a wilderness. There were no towns nearby. The few people living there were miners or loggers. Today, there are paved roads and electric lights around Mount Rushmore. The area is still wild, however. Mountain goats, buffalo, and elk roam nearby.

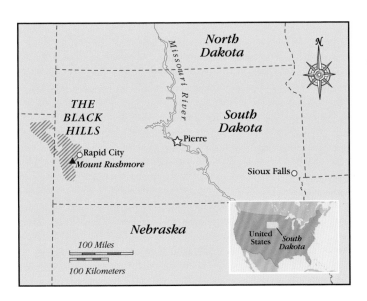

Mount Rushmore is located in the beautiful and rugged Black Hills in southwestern South Dakota.

Mount Rushmore is in the Black Hills of South Dakota. This area is in the southwestern part of the state. The closest large town is Rapid City. Mount Rushmore is important to the 61,000 people who live there. Many tourists use the hotels, stores, and restaurants in Rapid City. Mount Rushmore is the state's most famous tourist attraction. About 3 million people visit Mount Rushmore every year. As a national memorial, it is managed and run by the National Park Service.

Mount Rushmore in the Movies

Two major movies have featured Mount Rushmore. *North by Northwest* came out in 1959. In it, a gang of foreign spies think a businessman is a secret agent. In one famous scene, a fight takes place on top of Mount Rushmore. (The scene was not really filmed there. It was filmed on a large model of the mountain.) *National Treasure: Book of Secrets* was made in 2007. In this film, a man looks for secrets about the death of Abraham Lincoln. He finds a clue in a book. It says a city of gold is hidden inside Mount Rushmore and the sculptures were carved to hide the secret entrance to the city.

Gutzon Borglum (center), the sculptor who created Mount Rushmore, talks with workers putting the finishing touches on a presidential eye.

Four Faces

Gutzon Borglum was a **sculptor**. He created the Mount Rushmore sculpture. He chose the four faces that were carved on the mountain. Each president was chosen because he represents a key time in American history. Washington represents the founding of the United States and its fight for independence from Great Britain. Jefferson wrote the Declaration of Independence, and he also represents American **expansion**. When he was president, he purchased the Louisiana Territory from France. The Louisiana Purchase doubled the size of the United States. Lincoln represents the preservation of the United States. He was president during the **Civil War**, when the country was nearly torn apart. Roosevelt represents the United States in the early twentieth century, when he helped make the country into a world power.

A Shrine to Democracy

Mount Rushmore is a memorial. It is also a grand work of art and a major tourist attraction. The mountain is important for more than just those reasons, however. Mount Rushmore also represents American freedom and the country's **heritage**. The memorial represents what Abraham Lincoln called "government of the people, by the people, and for the people." Lincoln Borglum, the sculptor's son, once said, "the mountain today is...a **shrine** to **Democracy**." That is the importance of Mount Rushmore.

Photographs of Mount Rushmore

Lincoln Borglum was Gutzon Borglum's son. In the 1930s, while work on the monument was going on, he became Mount Rushmore's official photographer. The Eastman Kodak Company was trying new kinds of cameras and color film at that time. It sent samples of each to Lincoln. He took a great many pictures. Today, they are a history of the work on the sculpture.

The Black Hills

The first people to live near where Mount Rushmore is located were Native Americans. They came from Minnesota. Other tribes there called them *Nadouessioux*, which means "enemies." The name was shortened to Sioux.

Paha Sapa

The Sioux traveled west, across the plains of what is now South Dakota. They reached a place with high hills and mountains, covered with dark pines. The Sioux called the place *paha sapa*. This means "hills of black." The Sioux believed that the Black Hills were sacred (blessed or holy). They did not live, hunt, or fish there.

In 1743, two French fur trappers became the first white men to visit the area. Their Native American guides respected the Sioux's beliefs. They would not take the French trappers into the Black Hills. In the early 1800s, however, other trappers, soldiers, and miners did go into the Sioux's sacred ground.

In 1874, the U.S. Army sent troops to investigate the area and find a place to build a fort. The troops were led by Lieutenant Colonel George Armstrong Custer. They reported that there was gold in the Black Hills. White people rushed into the area. Towns like Deadwood sprang up almost overnight. By 1875, 10,000 whites were living in or near the Black Hills.

The Sioux fought to stop the miners and settlers. The U.S. Army was brought in to protect them. Battles were fought, with victories on each side. In the end, however, the Sioux were defeated. They were forced onto **reservations**. The U.S. government gave the Sioux money for the Black Hills. Some of their chiefs, however, did not want to take the money. To this day, many Sioux believe that the land is still theirs.

Dark-colored pine trees cover the hills and mountains around Mount Rushmore, which is why the Sioux named the area the Black Hills.

Attracting Tourists

South Dakota became a state in 1889. Most of the gold mines were closed by then. By the end of World War I in 1918, however, ranches, farms, and other businesses were growing. Doane Robinson was head of the South Dakota Historical Society. He was proud of his state's history and the beauty of the Black Hills. He wanted to bring more tourists to South Dakota.

Robinson read about a project near Atlanta, Georgia. Near the city was a huge rock wall called Stone Mountain. The sculptor Gutzon Borglum was carving giant figures of Civil War heroes on its side. People were flocking to see it. Robinson thought the same thing could happen in South Dakota.

Before the Mount Rushmore sculpture was started, an earlier plan was to carve standing figures of American heroes into the rock towers known as The Needles.

Red Cloud (1822–1909)

Red Cloud was a Sioux leader. In 1866, the U.S. Army began building forts on Sioux land to protect white settlers. Red Cloud led his men in a war against the army. After two years of fighting, Red Cloud won. In 1868, the U.S. government agreed to close the forts and keep off Sioux land. Red Cloud is known as the only Native American leader ever to win a war with the United States. In 1874, however, gold miners began rushing into the Black Hills. Red Cloud knew he could not stop them. Other Sioux fought then, but Red Cloud did not.

In this painting, Sioux warriors led by Red Cloud defeat the U.S. Cavalry in an 1866 battle.

He knew of some tall rock towers called The Needles. He imagined them carved into standing figures of western heroes. Robinson thought about statues of Meriwether Lewis and William Clark, who had explored the wilderness, including a large part of the Louisiana Purchase, for the U.S. government in 1804 and 1805. Robinson thought about the Wild West showman Buffalo Bill Cody and Chief Red Cloud, a great Sioux leader.

In August 1924, Robinson sent a letter to Borglum. Robinson wrote, "in the Black Hills of South Dakota are opportunities for heroic sculpture.... Would it be possible for you to design and supervise a massive sculpture there?" Within days, Borglum sent a telegram in reply. Borglum wrote, "Much interested in your proposal.... Can get to Black Hills during September."

Naming a Mountain

In 1884, a New York City lawyer went to South Dakota. He had to check the legal titles (ownerships) on some land. The lawyer hired a guide named Bill Challis to show him around. The lawyer asked Challis the name of every place they saw. He finally asked the name of one large mountain. Challis said, "It never had a name, but from now on we'll call it Rushmore." The lawyer's name was Charles E. Rushmore.

Garden of the Gods

Borglum arrived with his 12-year-old son, Lincoln. Guides helped them search the Black Hills to find good places for sculptures. There were no roads in the area. They had to explore on horseback and on foot. When Borglum visited The Needles, he found that the rock was not good for carving. The nearby Harney Range of mountains was much better. Borglum said its canyons, caves, and cliffs were "a garden of the gods." The Harney Range, however, was in both a national forest and a state park. To carve anything there, permission would be needed from both the **federal** and the state governments. That would take time.

The Mount Harney Memorial Association

Doane Robinson knew that carving a big sculpture would cost a lot of money. He formed the Mount Harney Memorial Association in 1925. This was a group of businessmen and ranchers. The group's goal was to raise money for the project. Peter Norbeck, a U.S. senator from South Dakota, joined the group.

While Robinson was thinking about money, Borglum was thinking about faces. Borglum loved the West. He did not like Robinson's idea of

Gutzon Borglum (1867–1941)

John Gutzon Borglum was born in Idaho on March 25, 1867. His parents were from Denmark. Borglum loved to draw, especially western subjects like cowboys and horses. In his teens, he ran away from home. He studied art in San Francisco, California, and went on to study in France, England, and Spain. Borglum changed the type of art he created from drawings and paintings to sculptures. He was especially interested in the human face. Borglum once carved a marble head of Abraham Lincoln. It is now in the Capitol building in Washington, D.C. (This is the building where Congress meets.) In 1915, Borglum started work on Stone Mountain, in Georgia. This sculpture would honor southern Civil War heroes.

Borglum was not an easy man to work with. When it came to his art, he had to have his own way. Work on Stone Mountain had to be put aside during World War I. Borglum began to work on it again in 1923. Two years later, he was fired. By then, however, he had agreed to work on Mount Rushmore. That project would fill the rest of his life. There, he also argued with the people who hired him. Borglum rarely thought about cost or time. He was concerned only with his art. In 1941, he was on his way to Washington to request more money for Mount Rushmore. He never got there. Borglum became ill in Chicago. He died there on March 6.

Before the Mount Rushmore project, Borglum had worked on the Stone Mountain sculpture in Georgia (right), which honors southern Civil War heroes.

A Woman's Face on the Mountain?

At one point, it was possible that a woman's face would also be carved on the mountain. Susan B. Anthony (1820–1906) had worked hard to get women the right to vote. Many people wanted Borglum to carve her face on Mount Rushmore. In 1937, Congress was asked for money to add Anthony's head. Congress said no. The government would pay only for the four heads already in progress.

carving just western heroes, however. He thought the sculpture should represent the whole country. Borglum decided to carve the faces of presidents into the rocks of South Dakota. He chose George Washington, Thomas Jefferson, Abraham Lincoln, and Theodore Roosevelt.

"On Each Other's Shoulders"

Borglum returned to the Black Hills in the summer of 1925. Lincoln, now 13, was with him. A guide took them back to the Harney Range. One day, they came to a high, gray mountain. Lincoln said later that it was "[what] my father had been searching for: a gigantic mountain of solid **granite**, towering above the surrounding peaks." Better still, it faced south. That meant that it would be in sunlight all day long. The mountain was called Mount Rushmore.

But was the stone good for carving? There was only one way to tell. They had to climb the mountain. They took ropes from their horses' saddles and started up. Lincoln Borglum described the climb:

"Scaling Mt. Rushmore was no easy task. The last 150 feet [46 meters] were almost **perpendicular**…. At one point we [stood] three men on each other's shoulders so the top man could loop his **lariat** over a [piece] of rock…. We reached the top—6,000 feet [1,830 meters]

Gutzon Borglum places an American flag at the top of Mount Rushmore during a ceremony to mark the start of the sculpture project in 1925.

above sea level and a good 500 feet [150 meters] above all the surrounding cliffs."

The climbers carefully examined the face of the mountain as they went up. They brought down samples of rock. Borglum spent two more days at Mount Rushmore. He took photographs of it from different places and at different times of day. In the end, Borglum was certain this was the place to carve his sculpture.

A Ceremony at the Site

Doane Robinson was very pleased. Senator Norbeck was less certain. He thought Mount Rushmore was too far out in the wilderness. There were no roads. Building them would cost a lot of money. Borglum finally convinced Norbeck that Mount Rushmore was the best place.

A **ceremony** was held at the site. On October 1, 1925, about 3,000 people gathered at Mount Rushmore. Bands played. Huge flags were raised on top of the mountain. Native Americans danced. Robinson and Norbeck each made a speech. So did Borglum. He told the crowd that the first head—George Washington—would be finished in one year. Borglum was wrong. Actually, it would be almost two years before work even started on the mountain.

Chapter 3

The Project Begins

The biggest problem in starting Mount Rushmore was money. The Mount Harney Memorial Association raised some. Borglum said his wealthy friends would make donations (contributions). Charles E. Rushmore also sent money to the project. The man for whom the mountain was named gave $5,000 to help carve the memorial. Even so, only a small amount of money was collected.

The President's Vacation

In the spring of 1927, the project got some help. The assistance came from a source no one expected: the president of the United States. Calvin Coolidge said that he would spend his summer vacation in the Black Hills near Mount Rushmore. That created interest in the area. The news brought in a lot of donations, too. The money that came in was put to use right away.

President Calvin Coolidge (center) visited Mount Rushmore on horseback during his 1927 trip to the Black Hills. The visit helped raise money for the sculpture.

Borglum bought a **generator** to make electricity. He set it up in an old mining town called Keystone. Power lines were run for 3 miles (5 kilometers) from there to the mountain. The electricity was needed for the **jackhammers** that would carve the mountain.

A cookhouse was built to prepare food for the workers. An old log cabin was fixed up for Borglum to use as a studio. A blacksmith shop and tool sheds were built, as well as bunkhouses where workers could sleep. At the top of the mountain, shelters were built to hold tools and supplies. They would also protect workers from storms. At first, everything—the lumber, cement, and machinery—had to be carried up the mountain by hand. Later, a long wooden staircase was built.

On August 10, 1927, President Coolidge arrived in Keystone. From there, he rode a horse to Mount Rushmore, where he made a speech. Borglum

A Unique Salute

The organizers of the 1927 ceremony wanted a big welcome for President Coolidge. They wanted to fire a 21-gun salute. They could not get soldiers or cannons, but they had a lot of dynamite. They also had a lot of tree stumps that had to be cleared. Explosives were put under the stumps. When the president arrived, the dynamite was set off. Calvin Coolidge may be the only president in U.S. history to get a "21-stump" salute.

then drilled the first holes in Mount Rushmore. The sculpture project was under way at last.

Borglum's Pointer System

A writer once asked an artist if sculpture was difficult. The artist replied, "No, it's easy. You just get a block of stone and chip away the parts you don't want." Gutzon Borglum's block of stone was a whole mountain. He had to find a way to identify the parts to "chip away." He also had to find a way to do the chipping.

Borglum carved a model of the giant sculpture he was planning. The heads on the model were 5 feet (1.5 meters) high. That was one-twelfth of the size they would be on the mountain. Next, Borglum built a device he called a pointer. It had a gauge for measuring angles. A long arm stuck straight out from the pointer. Borglum put the pointer on top of his model. Strings with small weights were hung from the arm. He measured points on his model based on the string. He noted how far each point was from the string, whether up or down or side to side.

Then, Borglum built a much larger pointer on top of the mountain. This pointer was first set up on the spot that would be the top of George

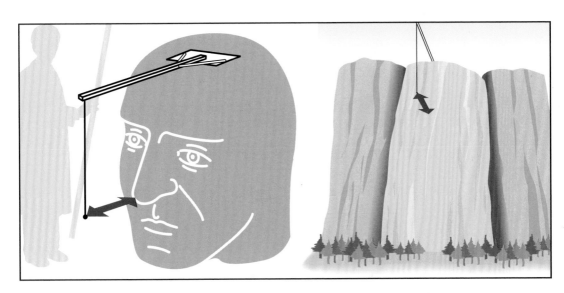

To figure out how much to carve out of the mountain, Borglum first made measure-ments, using his pointer device, on a model one-twelfth the size of the final sculpture. Then, he multiplied by 12 when measuring with a second pointer on the mountain itself.

George Washington (1732–1799)

George Washington was a farmer and a soldier. He was born in Virginia in 1732 to a wealthy family. When he was a teenager, he became a **surveyor**. Then he fought with the British Army against the French during the French and Indian War (1754–1763). Years later, when the American colonies began their war for independence against Britain in 1775, Washington was asked to lead the American army. He agreed, but he would not take any pay. "I do not wish to make any profit from it," he said. After some hard defeats, Washington led the army and the new nation to victory. He then went back to his farm and family.

Washington was called to service again in 1787. He led the meetings where the U.S. **Constitution** was written. In 1789, he was elected the country's first president. He served for two terms, from 1789 to 1797. He kept the United States at peace and helped the young country grow. Washington died two years after leaving office. Another Virginian, Henry Lee, wrote that Washington was "First in war, first in peace, first in the hearts of his countrymen." His face was the first one carved on Mount Rushmore.

Borglum uses one of the bosun's chairs set up for his workers to look at the scultpure's progress.

Washington's head. Borglum used his small pointer in the studio to make measurements. These measurements were taken to the large pointer on the mountain. The measurements were multiplied by 12. Marks were painted on the mountain based on those measurements. That identified the rock to be chipped away. Doing the "chipping" was more difficult. This work required drilling and dynamite.

Drillers and Call Boys

Each driller had to work in a special seat, which was called a bosun's chair. The chair was made of leather. Straps went around the worker's legs and waist. The bosun's chair was hooked to a strong steel cable. The cable was connected to a **winch** located in a shack on top of the mountain. After workers strapped themselves into the chairs, they hooked their jackhammers to the cable. Then they were lowered down the face of the mountain. They often worked 1,000 feet (300 meters) above the ground. One worker said, "It scared me…. You could look down and see just where you'd fall to, and it looked so far."

Drillers in bosun's chairs could move short distances to the left or right. To go up or down, however, they had to be raised or lowered by the winch. The drillers were a long way from the winch operators. They could not see or talk to them. Other workers, known as "call boys," were also lowered down the mountain, and they stopped about halfway

This driller stands on a wooden platform to make holes for dynamite in the side of the mountain. Other workers, called powder monkeys, then placed sticks of dynamite in the holes.

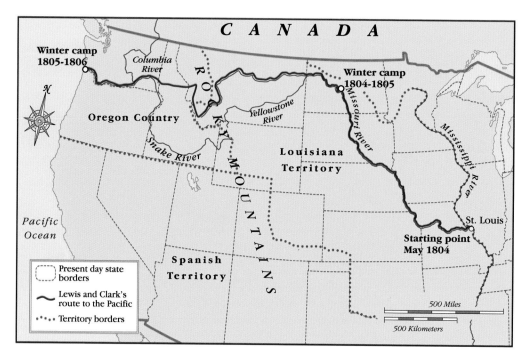

Lewis and Clark traveled for thousands of miles over more than two years to explore the Louisiana Territory purchased by President Thomas Jefferson and go beyond it all the way to the Pacific Ocean.

between the winch shack and the drillers. If a driller needed to go down, he would yell to the call boy. The call boy would then holler up to the winch operator, who would let out the cable.

Powder Monkeys

To remove large amounts of rock, holes were drilled about 6 inches (15 centimeters) apart. The holes were 3 to 4 feet (1 to 1.2 meters) deep. Once all of the holes were drilled in a marked area, the drillers were winched up. Then the dynamite men—who were called "powder monkeys"—were lowered down the face of the mountain. They placed sticks of dynamite inside the drilled holes. All of the dynamite was connected with electrical wire. The powder monkeys were then winched back up.

Thomas Jefferson
(1743–1826)

Thomas Jefferson was a gifted writer, but a clumsy public speaker. He was a farmer, a lawyer, and an **architect**. He loved science and reading. He played the violin and spoke several languages. Jefferson was born in Virginia in 1743 to a wealthy family. In 1776, he wrote the Declaration of Independence, stating the reasons why the American colonies believed they had to be free and independent from Great Britain. During the American Revolution (1775–1783), Jefferson served in the Virginia legislature, and he was the governor of Virginia for two years. In 1789, when George Washington became president, he named Jefferson secretary of state. Jefferson was elected vice president in 1796 (when John Adams was elected president).

In 1801, Jefferson became the third president of the United States. He served from 1801 to 1809. While president, in 1803, Jefferson made the Louisiana Purchase, buying a huge piece of land from France. The land stretched from the Mississippi River to the Rocky Mountains. This doubled the size of the United States. Jefferson chose Meriwether Lewis and William Clark to explore the land. Leading a group of about 50 people, Lewis and Clark spent more than two years traveling and mapping the area, as well as land farther west, all the way to the Pacific Ocean.

After leaving office, Jefferson spent the rest of his life farming, studying, inventing, and reading. His personal library had thousands of books. Jefferson died on July 4, 1826—the fiftieth anniversary of the Declaration of Independence. (In an interesting coincidence, John Adams died on the same day.) Jefferson's was the second face carved on Mount Rushmore.

The nearly completed head of George Washington, the first one to be carved, is shown in this photo from the early 1930s.

When the dynamite was set off, tons of stone were blown from the face of the mountain. Borglum planned each explosion carefully. Each time, he tried to blast away only half of the rock he wanted to remove. Borglum knew he could remove more rock later. He could not put it back, however, if he blasted away too much.

Drilling and blasting went on all through the summer and fall of 1927. By the time work stopped for the winter, Washington's head and face were beginning to take shape. There was a problem, though. The money for the project had run out.

Matching Money

Senator Norbeck went to work in Washington, D.C. He got Congress to pass a bill in February 1929. The bill made Mount Rushmore a national memorial. The new law also set up a new group to oversee the project. The group was called the Mount Rushmore National Memorial Commission, and it replaced the Mount Harney Memorial Association. The commission had twelve members appointed by the president of the United States. (Doane Robinson wanted to be one of them, but he was not selected.)

The new law also said the U.S. government would match any money that people raised for the monument, up to a total of $250,000. Congress began by matching the money that had already been raised. The first payment was almost $55,000, and this meant that work on the mountain was able to start again in the spring of 1929.

Interest in Mount Rushmore was growing. By the spring of 1930, 400 tourists were visiting Mount Rushmore every day. By summer, Washington's head was nearly finished, and Jefferson's head was under way. A dedication ceremony for Washington's figure was held on July 4, 1930. As winter approached, however, the project ran out of money once again.

"It Looks Very Well"

In 1930, the United States was in an economic crisis known as the Great Depression. Factories closed. Banks failed. Millions of people lost their jobs and homes. The Depression was not a good time to raise money to carve a mountain. Little work was done on Mount Rushmore from 1930 to 1932, and everyone was frustrated. Late in 1932, help came from Washington, D.C. Once again, Senator Norbeck was able to get some money to start work again.

Workers were glad to have jobs at Mount Rushmore during the Depression. Compared to other kinds of work at that time, the pay was good. The drillers were paid 75 cents an hour. The powder monkeys got $1 an hour. The carvers got $1.25.

Changes

When work began again in 1933, a major problem had to be fixed. Jefferson's head was being carved to the left of Washington's

Jefferson's head, partially completed in this photo, was the second one to be carved. At first it was to be to the left of Washington's. The stone was not good enough, though, and the head had to be moved to the right.

head. Workers had told Borglum that there was not enough good rock there. He did not believe them, but they were right. After a lot of work was done on Jefferson's head, it had to be blasted away. Jefferson's head was started again to the right of Washington's head. That is where it is today.

Another important change took place in 1933. Mount Rushmore was placed under the control of the National Park Service. The Park Service made a lot of improvements. A **tram** line was built to carry workers up the mountain. The Park Service also bought more equipment, fixed up buildings, and cleaned up the grounds.

Lincoln and Gutzon Borglum use the aerial tram built by the National Park Service to check the work on Jefferson's head.

Bumping

Throughout 1934 and 1935, workers carved Jefferson's head. Others blasted away rock to form Lincoln's head. Still other men smoothed Washington's face. As part of this "finishing" stage, small pieces of rock were cut away. No dynamite was used. First, Borglum marked the areas to be cut with red paint. Then, workers used small air-powered tools to cut and smooth the rock. The process of removing the last pieces of rock a little at a time was called "bumping." Borglum supervised the bumping very closely.

In 1936, 200,000 people visited Mount Rushmore. One of them was President Franklin D. Roosevelt. He came to see the dedication of Jefferson's head in August. The president made a speech. He also watched some of the blasting that formed Jefferson's face.

Abraham Lincoln (1809–1865)

Abraham Lincoln was born in Kentucky in 1809 in a one-room log cabin with a dirt floor. He was a champion runner and wrestler. He was a great storyteller. As a young man, Lincoln read everything he could. He once walked 20 miles (32 kilometers) just to borrow a book. He said, "My best friend is the man who'll get me a book." Lincoln became a lawyer in Illinois. He went into politics and worked to stop the spread of slavery.

In 1861, Lincoln became the sixteenth president of the United States. Only weeks later, the Civil War began. The North fought to bring back into the United States the states in the South that had seceded from, or left, the Union. (The Union was another name used at that time for the United States.) The 11 states in the South that had seceded all allowed slavery, and the future of slavery in the United States was one of the great issues of the war. In January 1863, Lincoln signed the **Emancipation** Proclamation. This document freed all the slaves in the parts of the South that were still rebelling against the United States.

In November 1863, Lincoln visited Gettysburg, Pennsylvania, for the dedication of a cemetery for Union soldiers killed in battle there. He gave a short speech that became famous. The speech, called the Gettysburg Address, used beautiful language to state what the North was fighting for. He ended the speech with these words:

> "[We] highly resolve that these dead shall not have died in vain—
> that this nation, under God, shall have a new birth of freedom,
> and that government of the people, by the people,
> for the people, shall not perish from the earth."

The Civil War ended in April 1865, with a victory for the North. Lincoln had succeeded in preserving the Union. Just as the war was ending, Lincoln was shot and killed by a southern supporter named John Wilkes Booth. A special train carried Lincoln's body home to Illinois. Lincoln is counted among the greatest American presidents. His was the third face carved on Mount Rushmore.

Rushing

Mount Rushmore was a difficult project to work on, but men doing hard, dangerous work can still have a sense of humor. Late one year, winter was closing in on the site. Everyone on the project was working faster, trying to get things done before the snow started falling. Signs were put up all around the site. The signs said, "Rush more!"

The Eyes of an Artist

By the end of 1936, Jefferson's head was nearing completion, and Lincoln's head was under way. In 1937, Gutzon Borglum turned 70 years old. His son, Lincoln, had joined the team years earlier. Lincoln was now in charge of most of the work on Mount Rushmore. Gutzon Borglum was still making all of the artistic decisions, however. The eyes in the faces are one example.

Borglum always studied the heads carefully. He looked at them from different places and at different times of the day. He watched the shadows and light. He made a decision about the eyes. The pupil of the eye—the black part in the center—is flat. Borglum, however, made the pupils in his sculptures stick out. Each one is 8 to 22 inches (20 to 56 centimeters) long. The pupils make shadows as sun moves across the mountain. The eyes look almost real.

The Hall of Records

In 1938, Borglum began work on the Hall of Records. This was going to be a huge cave filled with statues of 25 famous Americans. This project was very important to Borglum. He wanted it to honor American government, science, and art. Borglum planned to carve the hall into the back of Mount Rushmore. A grand set of 800 carved stone steps would lead up to it.

Theodore Roosevelt (1858–1919)

Theodore Roosevelt was a boxer, a cowboy, and a war hero. The teddy bear was named after him. Roosevelt—often called TR or Teddy—was born in New York City in 1858. His family was wealthy. As a young man, he was weak and sickly. He took up sports and outdoor living to make himself strong and healthy. In the 1880s, for two years, he owned a cattle ranch not far from where Mount Rushmore is today. During the Spanish-American War in 1898, Roosevelt became famous leading a group of soldiers called the Rough Riders. His fame helped get him elected governor of New York that year. He was elected vice president of the United States in 1900. When President William McKinley was assassinated in 1901, Roosevelt became the twenty-sixth president. At 42 years old, he was the youngest

president ever. While in office from 1901 to 1909, Roosevelt worked to control activities of big business that he believed were harmful to the country. He also protected American interests around the world. His motto was "Speak softly and carry a big stick" (which means: don't brag or bully but always be strong). Roosevelt pushed to build the Panama Canal, which connected the Pacific Ocean to the Atlantic Ocean. For these achievements, and many more, Roosevelt became the fourth face on Mount Rushmore.

Theodore Roosevelt's face on Mount Rushmore—the last one to be carved.

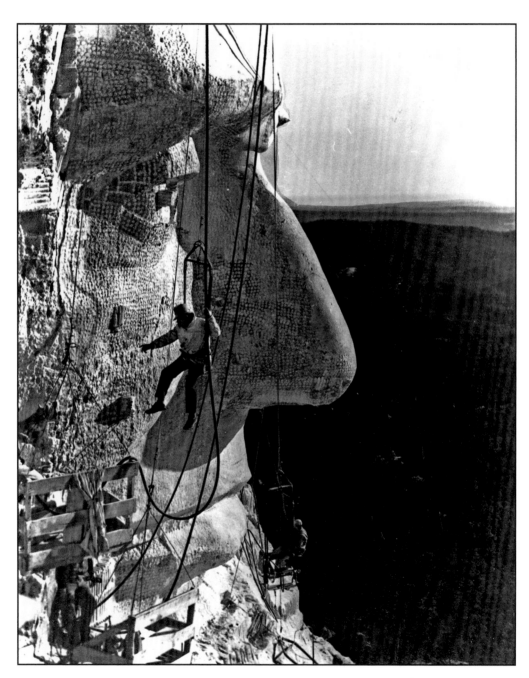

Abraham Lincoln's head was the third to be carved in the mountain. By 1936, a great deal of progress had been made on it, as shown in this photo.

Drilling and blasting for the hall started, but it did not go on for long. Two problems stopped the work. First, no one could remove the dust caused by drilling the cave. Workers were breathing in the dust, and they were getting sick. The second problem was an old one. Money ran out again in February 1939.

Finishing the Work

Borglum went to Washington to ask for more money. Congress set aside $250,000 to finish Mount Rushmore. The National Park Service would supervise spending it. After that, there would be no more money from the government.

The Hall of Records was never finished. In July 1939, however, Theodore Roosevelt's head was dedicated. The ceremony was held at night, with spotlights and fireworks. For the rest of that year and all of 1940, workers rushed to finish carving Roosevelt. They also did much of the final bumping on the other figures.

On March 6, 1941, Gutzon Borglum died. That summer, Lincoln Borglum directed the final work on the mountain. Roosevelt's face, Jefferson's coat collar, and Lincoln's beard were completed. Then the sheds on top of the mountain were torn down. All the machinery was removed. The tram was taken apart. The monument was declared complete on October 31. Lincoln Borglum's final report to the Park Service was made in November. He wrote, "I do not think any more…should be done on [the] figures of the Memorial. It looks very well as it is."

From 1927 to 1941, about 400 men and women worked on Mount Rushmore. During those 14 years, only two workers were seriously injured. Not a single worker died.

Lincoln Borglum became the first superintendent of the Mount Rushmore National Memorial. He held that post until 1944. He then moved

This photo shows Gutzon and Lincoln Borglum together not long before Gutzon's death in 1941. His son finished the Mount Rushmore project and became the first superintendent of the memorial.

to Texas, where he worked as a sculptor. Lincoln died on January 27, 1986.

Today, the National Park Service still maintains the monument. Every year, workers in bosun's chairs look for cracks in the sculpture. If they find any, they repair them. Until 1990, they used a special mix of granite dust and other materials invented by Gutzon Borglum. Today a waterproof elastic material is used. The material is then covered with granite dust to blend in with the sculpture. In 2005, the sculpture was washed for the first time.

It took 14 years to carve Mount Rushmore. It cost $990,000. Most of the money came from the government; $154,000 came from private donations. The largest single contributor was Gutzon Borglum himself. He once wrote, "Too little of it [civilization] lasts into tomorrow.... I want, somewhere in America,...a few feet of stone that bears witness [to]…the great things we accomplished as a nation."

This photo taken from an airplane shows the Mount Rushmore sculpture shortly before it was completed in October 1941.

Mount Rushmore will last for many, many tomorrows. It represents the great things the United States has accomplished. Most of the people who visit Mount Rushmore think that the Mount Rushmore sculpture itself is one of those great things.

The Lincoln Borglum Museum

There is a museum named for Lincoln Borglum at Mount Rushmore. It includes exhibits about the carving of the sculpture and a theater where visitors can see a short film about the memorial's history.

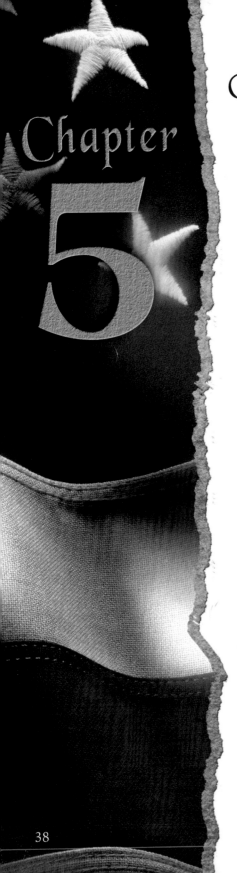

Visiting Mount Rushmore Today

Mount Rushmore is open every day except Christmas. Best of all, it is free! There is no charge to see this great monument (although visitors do have to pay for parking). Spring, summer, and fall are the best times to visit.

Flags, Trails, and Fireworks

Mount Rushmore has an information center, a restaurant, and a gift shop. Just past them is the Avenue of Flags. This walkway is lined with tall flagpoles. From them fly the flags of every state in the Union (as well as territories and districts). When a breeze is blowing, the Avenue of Flags is alive with color. Everyone with a camera takes a picture of it. At the end of the Avenue of Flags is the Grand Terrace. Many people think this is the best place from which to see Mount Rushmore.

There is much more to do at Mount Rushmore than just gaze at the faces. The

President's Trail is a half-mile (0.8-kilometer) walk with a lot to see and learn along the way. The trail starts at the Grand Terrace. It goes first to the Artist's Studio. This is the building where Gutzon Borglum worked. Inside you can see some of the tools that were used to carve the mountain. One of Borglum's large models is there, too.

Further along the trail is the Heritage Village. Here, you can learn about the history of the Black Hills and the customs and traditions of the Sioux people who lived there. The trail continues on to the base of Mount Rushmore. This is as close to the mountain as you can get. The President's

The Avenue of Flags leads to an area called the Grand Terrace, from which visitors can get a great view of Mount Rushmore.

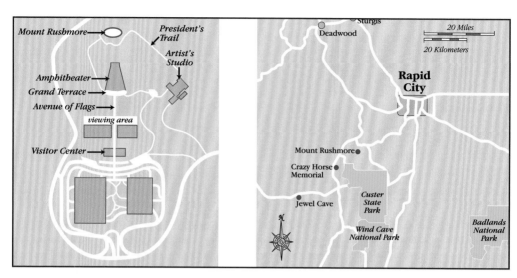

After touring Mount Rushmore, visitors can go to other sites nearby to enjoy the natural beauty and learn more about the history of the Black Hills region.

Trail then loops back to the Grand Terrace. You can walk the trail by your-self or join a "ranger walk." These are guided tours led by park rangers.

Near the Grand Terrace is the **Amphitheater**. There, on summer eve-nings, rangers give a talk about Mount Rushmore. A short movie is shown, too. Then, as it is getting dark, the lights come on. Mount Rushmore is lit up and shines brightly in the mountain night. If you visit on the Fourth of July, you will also see a spectacular fireworks show.

Other Places to See

The Black Hills of South Dakota have lots to offer. There are great things to see and do nearby after you have been to Mount Rushmore.

The Crazy Horse Memorial is a huge mountain sculpture of the Sioux leader Crazy Horse that is being carved near the town of Custer. When finished, the sculpture of Crazy Horse on horseback will be 641 feet (195 meters) long and 563 feet (172 meters) high. You can visit the site, which includes a Native American cultural center.

Crazy Horse (1842?–1877)

Crazy Horse was a Sioux warrior. He was respected by his people and feared by the U.S. Army. He fought to keep miners and soldiers out of the Black Hills. Crazy Horse was at the Battle of the Little Bighorn in Montana in 1876. The U.S. Army was trying to round up groups of Sioux and other Native Americans and force them to go to reservations. The Native Americans resisted. During the battle, Lieutenant Colonel George Armstrong Custer and more than 200 of his soldiers were killed. In 1877, Crazy Horse surrendered and was taken to a reservation in Nebraska. A few months later, he left the reservation without permission. He was arrested because the government thought he might be planning to return to battle. When he resisted, he was killed by a U.S. soldier.

A huge sculpture of the Sioux leader Crazy Horse is being carved into a mountain near Custer, South Dakota.

Each year on the Fourth of July, there is a spectacular fireworks display at Mount Rushmore, lighting up the impressive sculpture of four of the greatest American presidents.

Wild Bill Hickok (1837–1876)

James Butler Hickok was known as "Wild Bill." He was born in Illinois in 1837 and was a stagecoach driver and an army scout. He became a lawman in the 1860s. Hickok served as marshal in several rough Kansas cattle towns. He became famous for his long hair, fancy clothes, and skill with pistols. In 1872, Hickok joined Buffalo Bill Cody's Wild West Show. He left when gold was found in the Black Hills. Hickok ended up in Deadwood. There, in 1876, he was murdered while playing cards in a saloon.

Badlands National Park is east of the Black Hills. Millions of years of wind and rain have carved beautiful rock formations there. You can explore them by car, on horseback, or on foot.

Two of the world's longest caves are in the area. Wind Cave, at Wind Cave National Park, has about 110 miles (177 kilometers) of mapped passages. Parts of the cave are still being explored. In the surrounding national park, visitors can see bison and elk grazing on prairie grasses. Jewel Cave, at Jewel Cave National Monument, is even longer than Wind Cave. It is 143 miles (230 kilometers) long.

Deadwood was once a gold-mining town full of saloons, miners, gamblers, and gunmen. Today, you can visit a gold mine, take horseback tours, and explore several museums there.

Custer State Park offers camping, hiking, boating, and spectacular scenery. The park has an annual bison roundup. You can watch as 1,500 of these huge animals thunder across the prairie. Another kind of thunder can be heard in Sturgis. Since 1938, this small town has been home to a giant Motorcycle Rally every August. Thousands of riders show up each summer.

Timeline ★ ★ ★ ★ ★ ★ ★ ★ ★

★ **1867**   Gutzon Borglum is born in Idaho on **March 25**.

★ **1874**   Gold is discovered in the Black Hills; white settlers rush into the area.

★ **1884**   Mount Rushmore is named for lawyer Charles E. Rushmore.

★ **1924**   Doane Robinson writes to Gutzon Borglum about carving a giant sculpture in the Black Hills.

★ **1925**   The Mount Harney Memorial Association is formed. A ceremony at the site of Mount Rushmore is held on **October 1**.

★ **1927**   President Calvin Coolidge spends his summer vacation in the Black Hills. Work begins on carving the mountain.

★ **1929**   Mount Rushmore becomes a national memorial. The Mount Rushmore National Memorial Commission is formed. The Great Depression begins.

★ **1930**   Washington's head is dedicated.

★ **1933**   Lincoln Borglum becomes a full-time worker at Mount Rushmore. Jefferson's head is moved. The National Park Service takes control of the mountain.

★ **1935**   Work begins on Lincoln's head.

★ **1936**   Jefferson's head is dedicated.

★ **1937**   Lincoln's head is dedicated. Congress refuses to provide money to add Susan B. Anthony to the mountain.

★ **1938**   Work starts on Roosevelt's head and the Hall of Records.

★ **1939**   Roosevelt's head is dedicated. Work on the Hall of Records ends.

★ **1941**   Gutzon Borglum dies on **March 6**; Lincoln Borglum takes over. Carving ends on Mount Rushmore on **October 31**.

★ **1986**   Lincoln Borglum dies on **January 27**.

amphitheater: A building with raised rows of seats in a semicircle, facing a stage or an open area; amphitheaters are used for plays, concerts, and other events.

architect: A person who designs buildings and other structures and who understands how they are built.

ceremony: An event or set of actions to mark a special occasion.

civil war: A war between people of the same country.

constitution: A document that outlines a country's or a state's form of government and how laws are made and enforced.

democracy: A form of government in which power is held by all the people, who usually choose leaders to make laws and run the government for them.

emancipation: Freeing people from slavery or another unjust condition.

expansion: Getting larger.

federal: Related to the whole nation of the United States, rather than to the states.

generator: A machine that produces electricity.

granite: A kind of very hard rock.

heritage: Customs and culture handed down from the past.

jackhammer: A large power tool used for breaking up rocks or pavement.

lariat: A rope with a loop at the end that is used by cowboys.

memorial: A landmark or other place set aside because of its historic importance.

monument: A structure put up to remember a special person or event.

perpendicular: Straight up and down.

reservation: An area of land set aside for Native Americans to live on.

sculptor: A person who creates art by making shapes, like statues, often out of metal or stone.

sculpture: A figure or design carved or made from clay, wood, stone, or metal.

shrine: A place considered special because of past events that took place there or that it represents.

surveyor: A person who measures land to find its size and borders.

tram: A car, wagon, or container that hangs from an overhead cable and is used to transport people and supplies up and down hills.

winch: A machine with a large pulley and a cable, made for pulling or lifting things.

To Learn More ★ ★ ★ ★ ★ ★ ★

Read these books

Adamson, Thomas K. *South Dakota*. Mankato, Minn.: Capstone Press, 2004.

Borglum, Lincoln. *Mount Rushmore: The Story Behind the Scenery*. Wickenburg, Ariz.: KC Publications, 2006.

Calkhoven, Laurie. *George Washington: An American Life*. New York: Sterling Publishing, 2007.

Garraty, John. *Teddy Roosevelt: American Rough Rider*. New York: Sterling Publishing, 2007.

Mullin, Rita Thievon. *Thomas Jefferson: Architect of Freedom*. New York: Sterling Publishing, 2007.

Owens, Thomas S. *Mount Rushmore*. New York: Rosen Publishing, 2001.

Phillips, E. B. *Abraham Lincoln: From Pioneer to President*. New York: Sterling Publishing, 2007.

Temple, Teri, and Bob Temple. *Welcome to Badlands National Park*. New York: Child's World, 2007.

Look up these Web sites

American Experience—Mount Rushmore
http://www.pbs.org/wgbh/amex/rushmore

Mount Rushmore National Memorial
http://www.nps.gov/moru

National Geographic Society—Go West Across America with Lewis and Clark
http://www.nationalgeographic.com/west

South Dakota Tourism
http://www.travelsd.com

Key Internet search terms

Black Hills, Gutzon Borglum, Thomas Jefferson, Abraham Lincoln, Mount Rushmore, Theodore Roosevelt, South Dakota, George Washington

The abbreviation *ill.* stands for illustration, and *ills.* stands for illustrations. Page references to illustrations and maps are in *italic* type.

Index ★ ★ ★ ★ ★ ★ ★ ★ ★

★ ★

About the Author

William David Thomas lives in Rochester, New York. He has written books for children and young adults, software documentation, annual reports, magazine articles, speeches, and training programs. His four-book series *My American Government* received a Social Studies award nomination from the Association of Educational Publishers in 2008.